PETER AND PHILIPPA SCOTT'S

*Animals in Africa*

# PETER AND PHILIPPA SCOTT'S

# *Animals in Africa*

Clarkson N. Potter, Inc./Publisher

NEW YORK

Library of Congress Catalog Card Number: 63–17833

Text © Peter and Philippa Scott 1962
Photographs © Philippa Scott 1962
First published 1962 in London by Cassell & Company Ltd

Made and printed in Great Britain
by Jarrold & Sons Ltd

# Introduction

We offer this book about African animals as a contribution to the campaign for saving the world's wildlife. The campaign is gathering momentum, and it is world-wide in its scope. Many animal species, evolved over hundreds of thousands of years, have become extinct at the hands of man (in the last hundred years nearly a hundred kinds of birds alone), and scores of others are on the very verge of extinction. The prospect of species-extinction is, to us, appalling in its irrevocability. Animals which have taken all those millennia to acquire their unique and exquisite adaptations to their environment, now stand in imminent danger of being wiped out in a few decades because people do not care enough to prevent it.

There are, of course, wider aspects of conservation than the extinction of species. There is the whole field of renewable resources, the whole realm of ecology—that intricate relationship between water and soil, plants and animals, and man himself. It may be that a proper understanding of the Ecology of Man holds the secret of his very survival. Some think that threatened mammals and birds and reptiles are getting a 'free ride' on the wider issue of man coming to terms with his environment. But that is surely a materialistic view.

Supposing we ask ourselves two age-old questions: What are we here for? What distinguishes man from other animals? Do we answer the first as most other animals would—'To keep our bellies full and stay alive, at least until we have reproduced our species'? And do we answer the second by saying—'These things we can do more efficiently than other animals by reason of our well-developed brains'? Surely we must have higher ultimate aspirations. Should not our answers rather be that we know the difference between good and evil, and aspire towards good, that we recognize beauty and can strive towards it, that we have a continuing curiosity and must seek always for truth? No one can doubt that our values are wrong if we think only of material welfare.

For conserving wildlife and wilderness there are three categories of reasons: ethical, aesthetic, and economic, with the last one (at belly level) lagging far behind the other two.

The first argument arises from questions like this: 'Does man have the right to wipe out an animal species just because it is of no practical use to him, or is a nuisance to him? Are his belly-interests paramount? Is there an issue of right and wrong?'

'Supposing,' the argument goes on, 'that a man goes out and shoots the last Arabian oryx in the world, has he done something worse than if he had gone out and shot a Grant's gazelle or a wildebeest?' Many believe that taking animal life is morally wrong, but surely all would agree that killing the last individuals of a species is *more* wrong.

The ethical argument can be completed with the quotation from King George VI which hangs over the main entrance to the Nairobi National Park:

> *The Wildlife of today is not ours to dispose of as we please. We have it in trust, and must account for it to those who come after.*

The aesthetic case is a simple one: 'people enjoy animals; they find them beautiful and interesting, and often experience a re-creation of the spirit when they see them. To wipe them out is foolish and irresponsible because it deprives present and future people of a basic enjoyment. These arguments will not cut much ice with a man on a starvation diet. It takes a saint or a hero to put ethics (let alone aesthetics) before survival. To the large numbers of people in the world who are protein hungry, the economic arguments will inevitably be the strongest, even though they may be the least enlightened. But let those who are *not* hungry be quite clear in their minds that if conservation succeeds mainly on the economic case, man will once more, as so often in his history, be doing the right thing for the wrong reasons.

And what is the economic case? It rests on two main considerations—the tourist industry and food. Nothing is more certain than that travel will become cheaper and more popular, and that more and more people will flock to see the great wildlife spectacles of the world. Africa will assuredly draw thousands upon thousands to see the remnant—still a unique spectacle—of the great mammalian climax of the Pleistocene. A vast industry is waiting for development and it will bring riches to the countries which have taken pains to retain their wildlife.

Nowhere else in the world can one see—almost in a single eye-full—elephants, rhinos, giraffes, lions, zebras, wart hogs and perhaps half a dozen kinds of antelopes.

If you put capital into, say, a copper mine, in due course you are left with a hole in the ground, but if you conserve your wildlife you will draw revenue from it in perpetuity; it is a 'renewable resource'. At the same time the lives of thousands of people will be enriched by seeing it.

For the most part this wildlife will be in National Parks, and I hope and believe there will be new developments in the presentation of it to the visitor. Nowadays people usually watch from a vehicle, and in those Parks where the animals see enough vehicles to become totally accustomed to them, the watcher may see them living their lives undisturbed; but in most places the vehicle causes some interruption of natural behaviour. In future I believe the more sophisticated tourist may require some sort of observation hut or hide into which he can creep (a bus load at a time if necessary) and watch creatures which have no knowledge of his presence. Such observation huts must be accessible by a covered approach so that the watchers can come and go without making any disturbance at all. This may require some ingenuity to devise, but should not be wholly insuperable. Such hides, coupled with improved exhibits at the Park gates or at the Lodges, will give the Parks an even greater meaning to the visitor than they have at present.

But what of the wildlife outside the world's National Parks? Can it, too, survive? This is where protein considerations come in. It has been shown conclusively that on certain 'marginal' types of land a greater weight of protein can be cropped from wild ungulates (that is, hoofed animals), without detriment to the breeding stocks, than would come off the same acreage under domestic animals. Furthermore the wild animals, having a variety of slightly different feeding habits and food preferences, do not so easily damage the range in the way that domestic cattle do. Wherever this is true it is obviously wasteful and shortsighted to develop the land expensively for cattle.

Trypanosomiasis, carried by tsetse flies, is a serious disease in cattle, but the wild animals are immune to it, though the trypanosomes are in their blood. It cannot be sensible, on these vast areas of poor soil, to cut back the bush in order to get rid of the shade needed by the flies, and to slaughter the game in order to get rid of the reservoir of trypanosomes in their blood, when the protein derived from the cattle will be less than can be cropped from a healthy stock of antelopes. And in comparison, the risk of overgrazing will be substantially less under the wild species.

The conception of cropping wildlife is a sophisticated one which is not always easy to explain; yet it is likely to be necessary quite apart from the economic aspects. By comparison with former times, a sadly small proportion of the world's surface is nowadays available to wild animals. If we practise conservation for any of the reasons we have discussed, and if we agree that 'conservation is for man', then one of the prime objects must be to maintain, for the enjoyment of man, the greatest variety of animals and plants in their natural association; and this postulates a degree of 'management' of the various populations and habitats so that the common ones do not swamp the rare.

At the present stage of man's moral and physical evolution, it may be that in order to save wildlife we must stress the tourist industry and the protein; but there is one other factor less immediately commercial than either—the question of national prestige. Nature Reserves and National Parks have become a status symbol. A modern state is not complete without its chain of them and its enlightened code of wildlife legislation. Governments will continue to want their countries to appear modern, complete and enlightened. From this simple aspiration wildlife may yet derive additional security.

Recently Africa has been in the forefront of the conservation scene for a number of reasons, perhaps chiefly because of the sweeping political changes and because its wildlife is so striking and spectacular. Although only a remnant is left of the vast herds of mammals which formerly roamed the continent, yet in a few places the concentrations are still a staggering sight, both in numbers and variety. The birds, reptiles, amphibia and fishes of Africa are also astonishing in their beauty and diversity—and so, too, are the invertebrate animals, especially the insects.

Africa has its share of endangered species. The quagga and the blue antelope, like the dodo, are gone for ever. There is a long list of others whose continued existence is by no means secure —a list which includes both species of rhino, the mountain gorilla, the okapi, the cheetah, the red lechwe, the dibitag, the red hartebeest, the bontebok, the white-tailed gnu and the mountain zebra. For some of these rarities protection is already effective, indeed some only remain in semi-captive herds; but for others the situation is desperate.

In the conservation of threatened animals it is helpful to recognize two categories: first, those species which are limited by the available area of habitat remaining to them, and which will fill out this habitat against the current drain on their numbers, and secondly those which are limited by a mortality rate that exceeds their reproduction rate. Thus on the one hand there is a threat caused by habitat loss and on the other a threat by direct depopulation, in which every additional animal that survives is significant. The conservation measures are very different in the two cases. By far the most animal species are primarily controlled by available habitat, and this even includes most of the very rare species in Africa. The other category (which includes both white and black rhinos) seems to be a late stage in the process of extinction, calling for urgent action.

And this is not only an African problem. All over the world the evolution of man and his technology has spelled disaster for living creatures—by reducing their available habitat and by killing too many of them. Yet this same evolution has evolved conservationists—from the enlightened philosophies of some of the world's gentle religions to the modern naturalist who takes delight in watching the living animal and the modern ecologist who brings science to bear on the proper relationship between man and his environment. Conservationists today are involved in a gigantic holding operation—a modern Noah's Ark to save what is left of the wildlife and wild places, until the tide of new thinking begins to flow all over the world. That it already flows in some parts of it, is clearly indicated by the immediate response in many countries to the campaign of the World Wildlife Fund, and by the widespread interest in the work of the International Union for the Conservation of Nature—particularly its African Special Project, which offers technical help in conservation to the newly emerging African states.

As more and more people begin to think these issues are important, the threatened species will become increasingly secure. The time may not be far distant when all men will recognize the value of wildlife and wilderness to mankind, and will be agreed that these natural treasures must be preserved in perpetuity just as certainly as the great art treasures of the world. Then our tide will become a main stream in the evolution of man.

*Slimbridge,*
*Gloucestershire*
*April, 1962*

PETER SCOTT

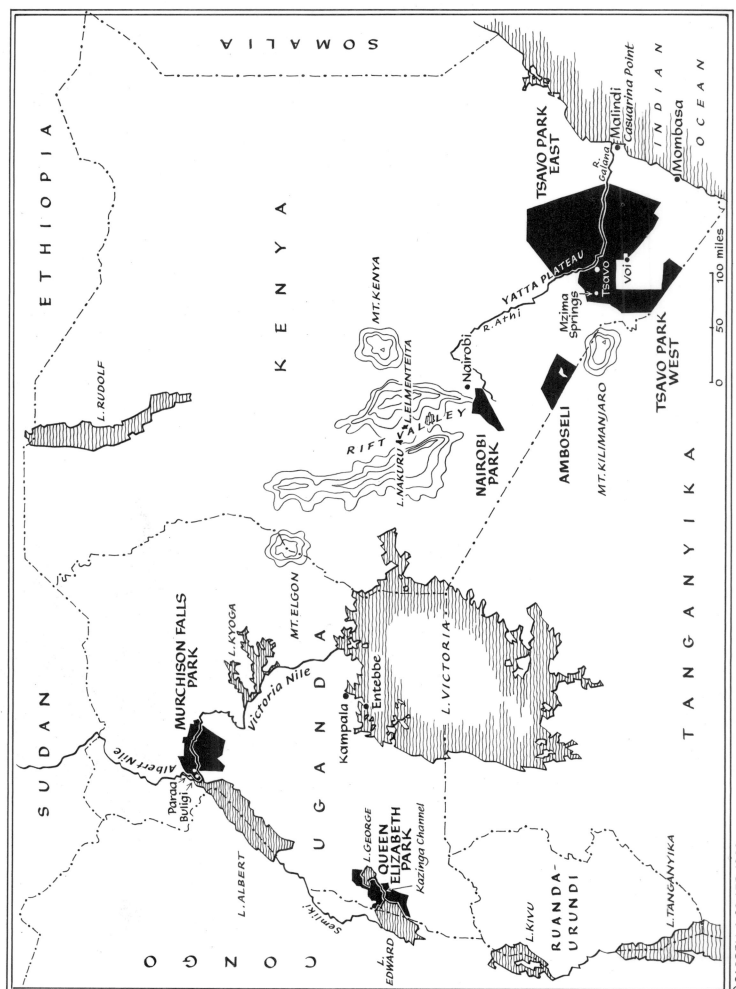

SOMALIA

ETHIOPIA

KENYA

SUDAN

UGANDA

CONGO

TANGANYIKA

RUANDA-URUNDI

INDIAN OCEAN

L. RUDOLF

MT. KENYA

RIFT VALLEY

L. NAKURU

L. ELMENTEITA

Nairobi

NAIROBI PARK

MT. KILIMANJARO

AMBOSELI

Mzima Springs

R. Athi

YATTA PLATEAU

Tsavo

Voi

TSAVO PARK EAST

TSAVO PARK WEST

R. Galana

Malindi

Casuarina Point

Mombasa

MT. ELGON

L. KYOGA

Victoria Nile

MURCHISON FALLS PARK

Albert Nile

Paraa

Buligi

L. ALBERT

Semliki

L. EDWARD

QUEEN ELIZABETH PARK

L. GEORGE

Kazinga Channel

Kampala

Entebbe

L. VICTORIA

L. KIVU

L. TANGANYIKA

0   50   100 miles

# Murchison Falls Park

# Murchison Falls Park

Among travellers there are those who believe that there is too much to see in the world to waste time going to the same place twice, and those who specifically enjoy going back to the same place year after year to bask in the nostalgia of it. Most often Philippa and I find ourselves exploring new places, but should one always deny oneself the very real and special pleasure of returning to a wonderful place after a lapse of time?

When the Trustees of the Royal National Parks of Kenya invited us to open a new National Park at Lake Nakuru in January 1961, and to see for the first time all the famous wildlife areas in that country, we could not resist the urge to break the journey in Uganda on the way, and revisit the Murchison Falls Park. Four years earlier we had been invited there to open the new Safari Lodge at Paraa on the north bank of the Victoria Nile, seven miles below the incredible Murchison Falls. Now our new excursion in Africa would begin with the pleasures of reintroduction, reminiscence, and reappraisal. All this would be the more enjoyable because the warden of the Park was an old friend, John Savidge, who had watched wild geese (and badgers) at Slimbridge as a boy. At the back of our minds was the vague fear that the place would not come up to our recollections. Had not the African wildlife situation sharply deteriorated even in the last four years? Would it perhaps all have changed for the worse?

Happily our fears were unfounded. There had apparently been extensive crocodile poaching (for the sake of their skins) but if there were fewer crocodiles, the difference was scarcely noticeable. To us the Park was as wonderful as it had been four years before.

The Murchison Falls Park consists of approximately 1,100 square miles of slightly rolling country bounded to the west by Lake Albert, and to the north by the Albert Nile. Through its southern half runs the Victoria Nile where the great river passes through a cleft in the rock only twenty feet wide. Seven miles below the Falls is Paraa, the Safari Lodge where you may stay in comfort among the animals.

The launch trip from Paraa up the river to the Falls is one of the world's most rewarding zoological experiences. Crocodiles and hippopotomus not always so easily seen in other parts of Africa are here in most impressive numbers. Elephants, waterbuck and, if you are lucky, rhinoceros are on the river banks. There are monkeys in the trees, great lizards which eat the eggs of crocodiles and soft-shelled turtles and a superb variety of waterbirds in the swamps. You will hear the wild cry of the fish eagle, and you will see something new each time you make the excursion.

In the foam-dappled pools below the Falls there are vast Nile perch, some of them weighing more than a hundred pounds—and swift elestes leaping and dashing in the spray.

But the river is not all. North from Paraa we found and watched and photographed Uganda kob, sturdy and ubiquitous, the graceful little oribi, long faced hartebeest, reedbuck, a rhinoceros with a baby and many elephants along the shores of the Albert Nile. We came upon a tree full of carmine bee-eaters and then more and yet more. At one point they were hawking round a group of elephants, exquisite in colour and form and movement, but not tame enough to photograph effectively without the paraphernalia of a hide, which was impracticable on so short a visit.

*Hippopotamus in the Victoria Nile*

*Day-old two-striped chameleon on hibiscus flower*

These huge creatures—related
to the pigs—spend most of the day
in the water; at night they come
ashore to graze. In some areas
they have become too numerous; for
example the country around the
Kazinga Channel in the Queen
Elizabeth Park became bare of
grass, as a result of overgrazing
by hippos, making it useless to
the other grazing animals such as
antelopes and buffaloes. Now a
harvest is successfully taken from
the hippopotamus herd; the
Africans are glad of the meat,
the grass has grown again, and
the antelopes are returning.
In the Victoria Nile the hippos
show no signs of permanently
damaging their habitat.

*Hippos making for open water—Victoria Nile*

*Flock of skimmers (Rynchops flavirostris) in flight—and on a sandbank in the Victoria Nile near Paraa*

*Nile cabbage*

This colony of about 325 skimmers was newly arrived since our last visit to the Murchison Falls Park. Their curiously shaped bright orange bills have the lower mandible much longer than the upper. They feed in flight, usually at dusk, skimming low over the water with the lower mandible just below the surface of the water. In the heat of the day they were clustered on a sandbank, often sitting back on their 'knees', which made their absurdly short legs look shorter still. On the same sandbank were several small crocodiles, and close by in the deeper water, hippos surfaced to watch us. We could get only so close to the skimmers as the draught of the outboard motor-boat would allow. As we ran aground about thirty yards away from them, they sat and watched us with surprising equanimity.

*Elephants by the Victoria Nile*

Of all the large animals in Africa, elephants are the most adaptable and successful in the struggle for survival. They can live in a surprisingly wide range of different habitats, but too often they come into conflict with man's interests. Elephants and agriculture do not easily coexist. And they are hunted, often illegally, for their ivory. Thus, over large parts of Africa, they are pushed back into the small remaining areas of national parks and game reserves in which they may well become too heavily concentrated. Too many elephants in a restricted area soon leads to permanent damage of the habitat. Branches and whole trees are torn down and do not have time to regenerate before the next lot of elephants comes along. The paradox is reached where these wonderful animals are so rare in some areas that every one should be preserved and so numerous in others that their numbers must be curtailed to prevent the disappearance of the forests, with consequent erosion and even change of climate, and of course, the disappearance of the elephants which caused it.

This is a sophisticated conception of conservation which is not always easy to convey to the layman either in Africa or elsewhere. It is an example of the complexity of the relationship between man and the other animals.

*Elephants at Buligi*

The first sight of a wild elephant can hardly fail to be memorable. No matter how many elephants you may have seen on film or television screen, the real thing in three dimensions in its wild habitat is vastly more impressive and exciting. Even if you are in a vehicle, which nowadays is the most normal way of seeing elephants in a National Park, there is still an element of risk. Some elephants ignore vehicles, but others still take exception to them. If the elephant is close to the road it is wise to wait until it has moved away, and this can mean a long delay.

*Cattle egret riding a large bull with more elephants near the river*

One Murchison Falls elephant decided to scratch his back on the radiator of a Land Rover and ended up by sitting down on the bonnet, which no doubt was unnerving for the occupants. At Paraa there was for many years a famous elephant called the Lord Mayor which lived around the Safari Lodge, and eventually took to overturning small motor-cars, apparently for the jolly noise it made.

One evening during our second visit there was, as there so often is, an elephant browsing peacefully at the foot of the slope below the lodge. We were disturbed by loud snorts and went to the edge of the terrace to find that an unwary photographer had wandered down in order to get a close-up photograph. He was now running for his life. Having seen him off, however, the elephant did not follow.

## Nile monitor

*Varanus niloticus* is a very adaptable reptile. It runs fast on land, it climbs trees, it swims well and dives freely—being able to stay under, it is said, for up to an hour. At the right seasons these great lizards live on the eggs of crocodiles and of soft-shelled 'turtles' which they dig out of the sand. Not far below the Murchison Falls we came upon three monitors digging up a turtle's nest. Two of them were already well fed, and made off as our boat approached the shore, but the third and biggest (he was about five feet long) was bolder. His greed overcame his fear, and he came back to continue digging out the eggs one by one, pausing for a moment when he had each in his mouth, and then swallowing it whole so that the bulge could be seen going down his throat. All the while we stood in the boat less than fifteen feet away.

*A male agama on the terrace*

*Paraa on the Victoria Nile*

The Lodge at Paraa consists of a main building with restaurant and a number of cottages with sleeping accommodation. All are beautifully thatched with papyrus. From the corner room of a new cottage specially built for the visit of Queen Elizabeth the Queen Mother, there is a superb view over the river. At dawn the flaming sky is reflected in the Nile, hippos grunt, fish eagles call, waterbuck and kob graze on the opposite bank, and an elephant drinks at the near river's edge. Spur-winged and Egyptian geese fly by. When the sun gets hot there are friendly agamas about the lodge. The males, with bright orange heads, blue-grey bodies and a patch of orange on the tail, sun themselves on the walls and in the garden; for every male there seem to be half a dozen dull brownish females or immatures. One female comes indoors to collect crumbs and sometimes sits sunning herself on the chairs in the hotel lounge.

A large plated lizard, *Gerrhosaurus*, which lived in a drainpipe at one of the wardens' houses turned out to be very photogenic. The pipe, disused, lay under a hedge and the lizard sunned himself just outside, retiring within at the approach of strangers. Hitherto he had always been treated with respect. No one before had ever blocked up the ends of his house and then dug it out of the soft earth. But this we did and pulled a small net bag over one end, into which the animal was persuaded to pop. After his tummy had been gently stroked while he lay on his back, he was quite prepared to play his part in our photography and grateful too no doubt to be returned in due course to his reburied drainpipe.

*A plated lizard (Gerrhosaurus)*

'Sausage tree' (*Kigelia ethiopica*), *by the Albert Nile*

*Portrait of a plated lizard*

*The fruit, about eighteen inches long, hangs on long stalks*

*Uganda kob at Buligi*

Kob are the most numerous of the antelopes in the Murchison Falls Park, although we saw plenty of oribi and Jackson's hartebeest as well, a few reedbuck and one bushbuck. Tantalizingly they all stand quite still and watch so long as the Land Rover moves, but the moment it stops they turn and gallop away. Kob do not occur much farther south than Uganda but have a wide range across the northern parts of 'Africa-south-of-the-Sahara'.

*Baby bushbuck*

*Female kob*

*The Albert Nile*

*Noctuid moth*

Four years earlier when we had visited the Murchison Falls Park the grass was so long everywhere that it was difficult to see the animals. Visibility was much better this time because of recent burning of the grassland. Rain had lately fallen and already the green grass was sprouting. But on a dry, burnt-up patch of bush with its hard spiky stubble we found a small noctuid moth clinging head downwards to a blackened grass stalk. Beautifully coloured in black, yellow and chestnut red, it matched its background perfectly, while the whitish stripe down the middle of its wings looked like a piece of unburned grass with a node. Man has burned the grass annually here, probably for thousands of years, and it seemed that this moth was specially adapted to escape detection on lightly burned rather than unburned grass. We disturbed it several times and it always settled in the same position at the top of the charred stems.

*Side-necked terrapin*

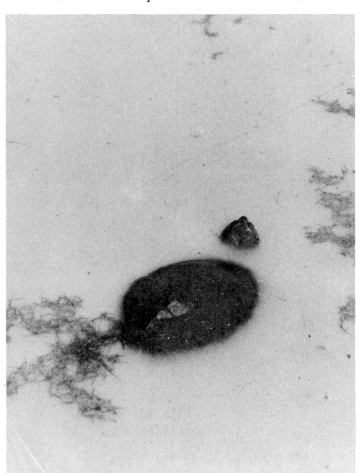

Crossing the track on the way to Buligi was a
side-necked terrapin in a surprisingly dry area.
We picked him up, photographed him when he
finally condescended to put his head out, then
took him with us to the next water hole, which
was a very muddy one. Side-necked terrapins are
a group which have too long a neck to protect
their heads simply by withdrawing it within the
shell, and get over the difficulty by folding the
neck sideways.

*Nesting pink-backed pelicans (Pelicanus rufescens)*

The drive from Entebbe to Murchison Falls Park takes about six hours but for a naturalist with a camera it may take much longer, because there are so many exciting things to see. A flock of pelicans nesting in a huge tree brought us to a halt. Large birds perched in trees always look comic and pelicans seem most incongrous of all. They had young, almost fully fledged and about as big as their parents, but they were not too old to be fed. Adults were arriving continuously from high in the clear blue sky, sweeping in at great speed, once round in a circuit and then down on to the nest in the thin topmost branches of the tree. We watched a young one plunge its whole head and neck down its parent's throat in characteristic pelican fashion.

*Marabou storks*

More irresistible large birds in a tree. This was the only tall tree within miles and it was full of nesting marabou storks. Some nests had half-grown young. By human standards the marabou is about the ugliest of birds, but the connotations of great age and decrepitude which their appearance suggests to us, are no doubt overlooked by other marabou storks.

*The forest canopy from above*

Just outside Entebbe there still remains one small patch of virgin forest. The Virus Research Institute has erected a tower there, one hundred feet high. From it the vertical distribution of mosquitoes at different times of the day and season have been charted and much has been added to the knowledge of their biology. We climbed to the top of the tower which is just above the canopy of the forest. Below us were small hornbills and bee-eaters and in the distance some red-tailed monkeys were playing. From the level of the canopy the huge trees were marvellously beautiful in the late afternoon sunlight.

## Hawk moths

These elegant moths with 'high aspect ratio' wings and heavy wing loading are marvellously adapted for high speed flight. They are the racehorses among moths.

Above is the huge chocolate brown *Nephele*, about the largest of the African hawk moths. Below, and much enlarged opposite, is the silver-striped hawk moth, *Chaerocampa celerio*, with pink hind wings, which has a world-wide range and has been recorded in Britain. In East Africa it is the commonest hawk moth.

*Colonial caterpillars belonging to the moth family Lasiocampidae*

*A young elephant, a young sittatunga and a very young bushbuck*

Orphan animals found by Park Wardens and Game Rangers can be a problem, but in Entebbe the Game Department has made a small zoo for them and gladly accepts any animals needing care. Without doubt the most enchanting animal in it when we were there was a baby bushbuck only a few days old. There was also a *very* tame sittatunga fawn and some buffalo calves, one complete with two oxpeckers which always managed to be on the wrong side of the buffalo's back and were very camera-shy. The sittatunga is rather a rare and shy antelope which is related to the bushbuck but is specially adapted for living in papyrus swamps.

The 'Elephants' Child' had a great liking for mangoes so we went in with a bucket, but he did not care much for strangers and finally charged Philippa as she was photographing him and pushed her back against the barrier.

*Conversation piece: Philippa and young sittatunga*

*Young male bushbuck*

*Buffalo calf with red-billed oxpecker*

*Buffalo calf*

*Young sittatunga*
As it walks it shows one of its enormously elongated hoofs which are a special adaptation to the floating swamp vegetation on which, in most areas, the animal spends its life.

*Carmine bee-eater at Buligi, Murchison Falls Park*

*Young crocodile*

*Egg case of grass mantis with young just hatched*

*Grasshopper (Tapesia)*

*Chamaeleo bitaeniatus ellioti*—male (left) and female

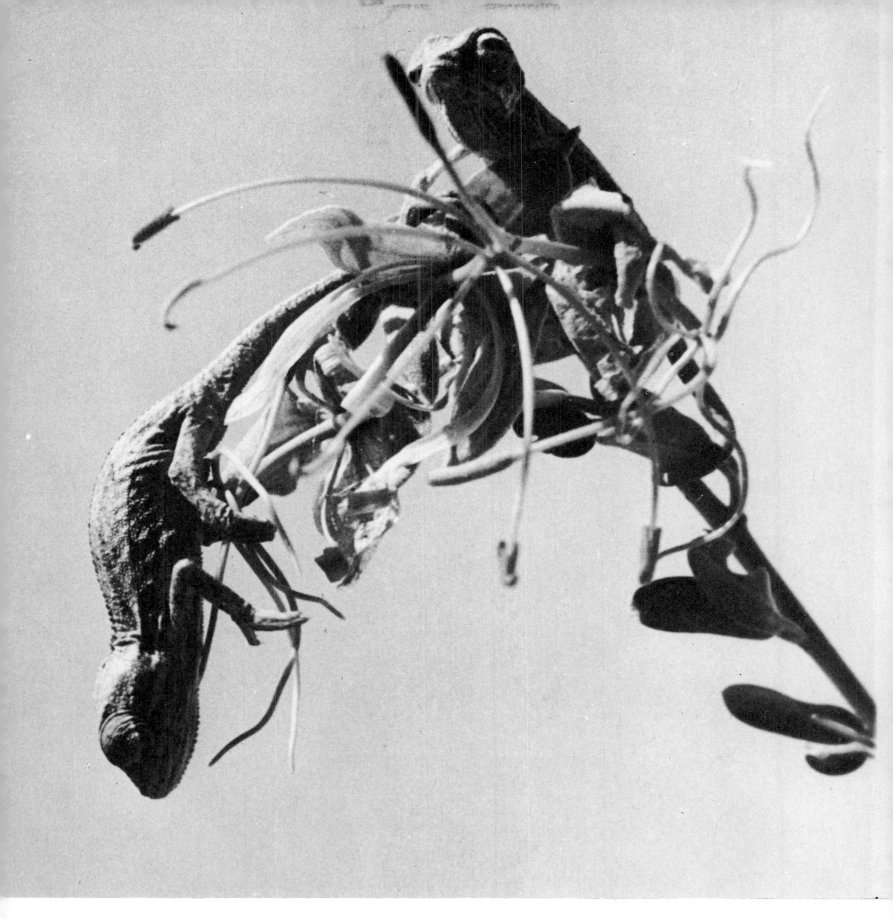

*Above: Newly born young of Chamaeleo bitaeniatus ellioti, five times life size*

*Left: The mother with four of her live-born young*

Philippa found a chameleon on the first day of our first visit to Entebbe and has found several since, but look as I may, I have never yet been able to find one myself. 'You just look in a bush' was the reply I got when I asked my old friend, Cecil Webb, how I could achieve this minor ambition, but although I have looked in many bushes I have had no luck. On our return visit to Entebbe however the African garden boys brought in about ten for us to photograph. The sun promptly went in and as we were leaving for the Murchison Falls Park early the next day we decided to select a few of the most handsomely marked ones and take them with us. They showed considerable individual variation. One green male was beautifully marked along his sides with a tortoise-shell pattern of chestnut brown. Another maintained a dark brown general colouring with a bright yellow stripe on his sides. Excitement seemed to make them first darken in colour then lighten to very pale yellowish green. This was also the colour if they got very hot. With the tail, this species does not seem to grow more than about five-and-a-half to six inches long. Ours became tame at once and, perched on our hands, would mop up flies from the windows. Two of the females were obviously about to have young and we included them in our luggage for the Park. On the second day one of them gave birth to eleven babies—all beige and very small. Two days later we released them all in the Entebbe garden.

# Nairobi Park

# Nairobi Park

'How sad that you should see it like this,' said Mervyn Cowie when we arrived at Nairobi. There had been no rain for nine months and the whole countryside was a pale burnt-up brown. But we had never seen herds of zebra or giraffes before, and we saw both as we pulled away from the airfield. The most striking feature of the Nairobi Park is that great herds of wild animals can live so close to a big city. The Park gate is almost at the city limits. The Park itself is small—only forty-four square miles—but the large numbers and astonishing variety of the animals are assured by the Masai Reserve which adjoins the Park to the south and acts as a great reservoir of game.

Owing to the drought hundreds of animals were dying in the Park when we were there in February 1961—especially wildebeest which were in the middle of their breeding season. The mothers had not enough milk for their young. The vultures were glutted and sat about idly while carcases rotted in the sun with an appalling stench. From afar one day we spotted a very small animal apparently chasing an adult ostrich across the plain. Interested, we set off to intercept them. On converging after a long and bumpy ride across the bush, we saw that it was a day-old wildebeest which had mistaken the ostrich for its mother. The ostrich, embarrassed, had trotted away and so the tragic little chase had begun. By driving the Land Rover between them we managed to cut the link of mis-conception, but there was no way of getting the little wildebeest to go back to where it came from, and anyway its mother may well have been dead or dying; nor could we catch it for human care.

Even while we were staying there, new water supplies were being installed in the Park and it was wonderful to see the animals finding the new water holes. But water was not the only problem; the drought caused food shortage too and the supply was now inadequate for the herbi-vorous animals. The lions and other predators were doing well, on the other hand. Lions are noble animals, and exciting to see, though I often think they enjoy a rather exaggerated popu-larity. For too large a proportion of the visitors to the Nairobi Park (and to many other Parks) they have become the be-all and end-all. The visit is held to be a failure if you see no lions. The numbers and precise whereabouts of the lions in the Nairobi Park are well known and many of them are known by name. A pride was marked down for us on our first day by a Ranger who had mysteriously disappeared by the time we got there in the Land Rover (which made us wonder if he had been eaten). The lions had recently killed and fed and were sitting about lazily in the hot sun looking gorgeously soft, sleepy and contented. They watched us carefully with their yellow eyes if we moved, but mostly showed boredom and disdain.

One evening we came upon a lioness with three cubs close to the road. The cubs were playing delightfully but we saw the lioness leave them by a small dam and purposefully slink away. Breathlessly we watched her pick a small party of wildebeest and stalk it in the dusk. Closer and closer she crept and we found it difficult to keep our binoculars steady. Vicariously we shared the suspense. Eventually, crouching in tallish grass and only just visible to us, the lioness seemed to be within fifty yards of her quarry and we thought she would make her final dash at any moment. But something went wrong; the wildebeest fled diagonally across her front and two minutes later they were a hundred and fifty yards away. The opportunity had gone. The lioness raised her head; that stalk had been a failure. In the gathering darkness we lit her with a spotlight from the car. She paid no attention whatever.

Nairobi Park has not only astonishing concentrations of animals but also a remarkable variety of different kinds which may be seen in company. Sometimes we saw seven species together at a dam or at a salt lick. Besides lion, we saw and photographed giraffe, zebra, eland, wildebeest, kongoni, waterbuck, impala, Grant's and Thompson's gazelles, wart hog, and a great many birds, from ostrich downwards.

Surely there must be a lesson to be learned from this Park where urban man and the wild animals live successfully side by side.

*A pride of lions*

During the preceding night they had killed a zebra, but in spite of that an unsuspecting baboon rustling through the bush attracts the attention of the two young lions. But they were too well fed to be bothered and the baboon went off at high speed when it discovered its proximity to danger.

One of the pride was an adult lioness, perhaps mother of the younger animals. She kept herself a few yards apart from the rest.

The young lions look out across the Mbagathi River Valley; but it will be a day or two before hunger drives them to kill again. Lions rarely kill in excess of their food requirements. This is normally true only of those few predators which can be virtually sure of a meal whenever they want it. A predator which has a struggle to catch enough prey may have an orgy of killing should the opportunity present itself, but in this the lion seems generally to be more moderate.

*Termites' nest engulfing a thorn bush—Tsavo East*

This lion, one of the two in the pride known in the Nairobi Park as 'the Spivs' is seeking the shade, even though it is eight o'clock in the morning. One of the difficulties in photographing lions, especially in the heat of the day, is that they can rarely be persuaded to spend more than a few seconds in sunshine.
On the next two pages are photographs of the other 'Spiv' and his lioness. All these pictures show the extraordinary way in which a stationary vehicle near them is completely ignored.

*Lion (one of 'the Spivs') in Nairobi Park*

*Eland*, the largest of the antelopes, the one most featured in the Bushman cave paintings, the one that has been used in recent experiments in wild animal ranching. They are, of course, more bovine in shape than the smaller antelopes, heavier and less graceful than their close relation, the kudu, but they have a special appeal. In spite of their heavy build they often leap skittishly like impala do. Their soft colouring is extraordinarily beautiful. The little black mark on the fore leg and the black tuft on the tail are presumably for quick species recognition so as to keep the herd together.

As an eland walks its hoofs make a curious clicking noise which can be heard more than a hundred yards away.

*Impala ewes in the shade.* It is hard to believe, when one sees a group like this without their ram (who was standing in the shade a dozen yards away), that these animals are only very distantly related to deer, which they resemble so closely. The requirements of a herbivorous animal are so similar in various parts of the world that they have become evolved from quite different Families to an almost exactly similar shape and colour.

*Kongoni*—one of the hartebeest group—
to our eyes less graceful than some other
antelope species. They are light fawn
colour and one of the commonest kinds
in the Nairobi Park. Opposite is a newly-
born calf.

Burchell's Zebra often associates with wildebeest (which are with them in the herd at top left). It is one of the most numerous of the 'plains game', a principal prey of lions, a beautiful intractable animal which has never been able to be domesticated.

The stripe pattern is never identical in any two animals.

*Giraffes at a dried-up salt lick in the Nairobi Park*

The giraffe above is licking and eating dried earth impregnated with salt. As when it is drinking it must spread its fore legs wide in order to get its head down low enough. The giraffe, a giant aberrant antelope, is often used as a prime example of the processes of evolution by natural selection. The long legs and long neck are obviously advantageous adaptations to a browsing animal finding itself initially in competition with other browsers. Once the leaves of trees have become your staple diet, the higher you can reach the more likely you are to survive a drought or other food shortage. Furthermore, once you have become so tall, it is an effort to get down below a certain height, which leaves the lower levels of the trees to the smaller browsers. It is a perfect example of an animal filling a particular ecological niche, and living in harmony with other species which have similar food requirements.

*Ostriches*—which are quite common in the Nairobi Park and are often seen feeding close to the grazing mammals. On the right is the day-old wildebeest which had lost its mother and then, thinking it had found her, had begun to follow the male ostrich. They must have run three miles or more by the time we cut between them and halted the lost calf. But we could not catch it, and its chances of survival were slender indeed. In this case its instincts had played it sadly false.

*Giraffe, wart hogs, kongoni and zebra at a water-hole in Nairobi Park*

*Impala ram with his ewes—Nairobi Park*

*The teeming ants' nests of the whistling thorn (Acacia drepanalobium)*

The whistling thorn carries galls which grow into small hard spherical chambers housing a particular species of ant. Some of the galls contain ant larvae and pupae at various stages of development, others are evidently used as storage chambers. In the Nairobi Park there are many thousands of whistling thorn trees, and in each many hundreds of galls. The numbers of ants involved make the imagination boggle.

*Ostrich, wildebeest, wart hogs and a yellow-necked francolin*

One of the most remarkable features of the Nairobi Park is the variety of species to be seen together. Here the wart hogs are demonstrating the characteristic feeding method in which they get down on their fore-knees which become especially calloused for the purpose.

*Jackson's three-horned chameleon*

This beautiful female chameleon was found by Philippa in Mervyn Cowie's garden just outside Nairobi. Its basic colour was grey-green with broad irregular-shaped vertical black stripes. From this it could change to pale yellow on the one hand, with or without the stripes, and dark brown on the other.

The notion that a chameleon can exactly match the colour of its background is an exaggerated over-simplification. Up to a point it can usually adopt a colouring best suited to conceal it, but basically the colour changes are related to the intensity of the light, the temperature, and the chameleon's state of mind. The colour and tone will change if the animal is afraid, or aggressive, or resting, or too hot, or hungry. In Jackson's chameleon there is one pattern for walking on the ground and another for climbing in a tree or bush.

*'Tikki', a tame female grey duiker —not a unicorn*

The male in this species has small horns, the female only the central tuft of hair, which can be seen well on the left and below on the right against her right ear. Tikki belonged to John Pearson in Nairobi and had been a household pet for four years; she was delightfully confiding. Although a common antelope in Kenya it is very seldom seen, keeping mostly to the thick cover.

Eagle owl, and African kestrel, brought up as pets by John Pearson and his family in Nairobi. Opposite, a young Woodford's owl.

# Tsavo Park

*Young banded mongoose*

A family pet of David Sheldrick, Warden of the Tsavo East Park.

# Tsavo Park

This great area of 8,000 square miles is divided administratively into two Parks—Tsavo West and Tsavo East. The Western Park, in the charge of Tuffy Marshall, is scenically magnificent but does not at present carry the great herds of ungulates which it might, partly because they had largely been killed off before the Park was declared and have not yet had time to re-populate the area, and partly because large expanses of potential grazing are out of range of water during the dry season. New bore holes and water troughs are being installed in order to open up these areas to the animals, and already this policy has been remarkably successful. The most astonishing natural feature of the Park is Mzima Springs, where a whole river gushes out of the ground into beautiful clear pools frequented by a herd of hippos, which can be seen lying in a pink cluster in midstream. There is an ingenious tank at the side of one pool into which one may descend by a ladder to get an underwater view. Sometimes the hippo can be seen from the tank, or a crocodile, but always a magnificent shoal of barbus, which look rather like chub. The largest must have weighed about five pounds. Around the pools is a lush vegetation including raffia palms and reeds and in the trees were vervet monkeys which make a good thing out of the tourists picnic scraps.

The elephants in Tsavo East were strikingly different from those we had seen in Uganda, for they were covered in the local red soil and looked almost chestnut-coloured. At the junction of the Tsavo River, fed by the Mzima Springs, and the Athi River, which was quite dry because of the drought, the two become the Galana River, along which we drove to a romantic camp, set up especially for us on an island in the river, under the shade of a grove of beautiful daum palms. The camp was opposite a cleft in the escarpment of the Yatta Plateau, and over this pass was a well-worn track made by the animals which fed in the waterless plain beyond. During lunch there was a cry of 'Elephants!' and we could see them in the far distance coming fast down the track from the pass, evidently intent on drinking. We took up a position on the bank in the shade and cover of a bush—seven of us including Mervyn Cowie, Director of the Parks, David Sheldrick, the Warden, his wife and six-year-old daughter, and Peter Jenkins the Assistant Warden—and there we waited for the elephants to arrive. They came to the far bank of the river just below us and only about fifty yards away, and at once they began to drink and to splash water over themselves, occasionally lifting their trunks to sniff the wind, on which perhaps some evidence of our camp and ourselves may have eddied towards them. In colour they were a delightful pinkish red because of the red soil in which they had been dust bathing. There were nine of them, including one quite small baby.

After nearly half an hour during which we watched them and took many photographs, one of the elephants crossed the river (there only about two feet deep) to our island, and the rest followed. Evidently they contemplated spending the afternoon in the shade of the daum palms. As they reached our shore and turned a little in our direction we began to withdraw and then the oldest cow saw us. She came determinedly up the bank towards us. At this stage we all began to run. David Sheldrick and Peter Jenkins turned and pelted them with daum palm nuts which had little effect as the elephants headed on towards our tents. But then, when they were about twenty yards short, they turned and skirted round one end of the camp, as David started up a Land Rover, revved the engine with a roar, and rushed them to speed them on their way. I do not really know how dangerous the situation was—if at all—but for a couple of minutes it was very exciting.

This camp provided us with some delightful animals to photograph, the most appealing of which was a young tame banded mongoose belonging to the Sheldricks; then there was an enchanting blue-grey dormouse brought in by one of the rangers. Less attractive but nonetheless fascinating were two huge scorpions which we dug out of their hole. The larger one was more than six inches long.

But most memorable of all at our Galana River camp were the elephants. After supper we went to the river bank again and saw eighteen of these magnificent pachyderms stretched across the silver track of the full moon which had just risen above the Yatta escarpment. They were no more than sixty yards away, drinking with stentorian sniffs and gurgles as they sucked the water into their trunks. At the waterside near by stood a black rhino.

From time to time during the night we got up to see the elephants and rhinos coming down to the water, drinking and going off again up the hill.

*The Galana River*

*Pink elephants*

Because of the colour of the soil, the Tsavo elephants are a glorious reddish colour. These had come down through the cleft in the Yatta plateau. After drinking they crossed the river and advanced unexpectedly into our camp under the bifurcated doum palm trees on an island on the Galana River.

*Elephants drinking in the Galana River—Tsavo East*

The party of elephants which bore down upon us and our camp and turned away only at the last moment.

*The beach at Malindi, with swift and lesser crested terns, sooty gulls and whimbrels*

They were pelted with doum nuts, which had little effect at first, but just before they reached the tents, the elephants turned away and made off at their best speed.

A black scorpion—
more than six inches
long, which filled the
bowl of a soup plate.

*Right:*
*An ant lion*
Above, the perfect
insect; below, the
larva which makes a
little pit of sand in
order to trap ants.
Once over the edge
they slither down the
slope to be seized by
the huge jaws of the
larva waiting hidden
at the bottom.

*The banded mongoose: young above, adult right*

This enchantingly playful young banded mongoose belonged to the Warden, David Sheldrick, and was completely tame. When given an egg he backed it up towards a tree trunk and then threw it backwards against the hard surface to break it. This is characteristic mongoose behaviour and must be innate as this one was hand-reared, and could not have learned it from his mother.

An exquisitely beautiful dormouse, *Claviglis murinus*, from the Galana River, rather slow moving and tame by nature.

*A dormouse, Claviglis murinus—Tsavo East*

Orphan black rhino calf, which was being bottle-fed by the Wardens at Voi in the Tsavo East Park.

*Male agama in breeding colour—Tsavo West*

*Vervet monkeys and a barbus*

These were photographed at Mzima Springs in the Tsavo West Park, where the fish can be viewed from a submerged tank in the river.

*Masai cattle*

The Masai tribe are pastoralists living on the milk and blood of their cattle; thus cattle have come to represent wealth and many Masai own far more than are necessary to feed them and their dependents. Overgrazing has followed and 'dust-bowl' conditions exist in large parts of Kenya and Tanganyika. The vegetation is destroyed, the top-soil blows away in the dry season and washes away in the wet. The land of Africa, already so poor in these areas, finally loses its capacity to produce food either for cattle or man. If they are to survive, the pastoral peoples of Africa must learn not to overstock their grazing, and science must be allowed to improve it for them. It is significant that far larger stocks of wild animals, capable of producing a much greater weight of protein per acre, can live on these poor soils without irrevocably damaging their habitat.

# Kenya Seashore

*Sooty gulls (Larus hemprichi) on the shore at Malindi*

# Kenya Seashore

Malindi is famous for its big-game fishing, but we went there for the much more exciting pursuit of 'fish watching' on the coral reefs. We stayed with Archie Ritchie—pioneer Game Warden of Kenya—now living in retirement at Casuarina Point opposite some of the most lovely coral gardens we had ever seen. His wife Queenie came goggling with us to show us the best places, with her dachshund, 'Voetsaak', either swimming alongside, or being towed on his own half-sized Lilo.

For a week we swam daily, hour after hour, identifying the fish species, watching and comparing their hehaviour, studying their very localized distribution on the coral, and marvelling at the diversity, the brilliant colouring, and the specialized habits of more than a hundred different kinds of fishes.

On a coral reef one can see a climax of fish evolution which is comparable to the climax of bird evolution to be found in a tropical forest. It was extraordinary how often we found ourselves drawing very precise parallels in evolutionary development, in behaviour and mode of life between fishes and birds. Here, under water, are the equivalent of rollers and bee-eaters and hoopoes, of wagtails and chats, of nightjars and owls, eagles and 'little brown birds'. Here one can find the same individual fishes in the same coral glades day after day, one can watch pairs at their courtship, aggressive males defending their territories, shy and retiring species peeping out from the cover of a coral 'bush'. By comparison with the study of birds fish-watching is in its infancy. Discoveries of great simplicity and perhaps considerable zoological significance are waiting to be made by any observer who knows how to be observant. I predict that because of the now widespread use of goggle-masks and snorkels, the science of ichthyology is on the threshold of great new discoveries, especially in the field of fish behaviour.

In our fish-watching we usually swim arm-in-arm or hand-in-hand, which ensures that whatever we find is seen by both of us, and we use a mask that covers the whole face so that we can talk to each other as we swim. On a coral reef most of the fishes can be seen very well from the surface, and we do not often find it necessary to dive down to get a closer look. We had no aqualungs at Malindi, and should scarcely have been better off had we had them. The magic begins as soon as the mask is lowered through the surface film. Although you are still breathing air through the protruding snorkel tube, you are in the fishes' world—a world not only of overwhelming interest to any naturalist, but of incredible beauty too. It is an experience which should not be missed.

Malindi was rich in all kinds of small creatures which the Africans call 'du-dus' and the Ritchies' garden produced a magnificent variety. The sea is encroaching on their property, and Casuarina Point is being gradually washed away. Efforts to delay the process have been made with wooden groins, and the stumps and roots of the fallen casuarina trees no doubt help to break the waves at high tide, as well as making a decorative foreground for a photograph. Already one building has been washed into the sea. We stayed in a delightful house at the very edge of the strand in which the Ritchies used to live; they themselves have now moved back eighty yards into a new house, more secure from the processes of erosion.

At Casuarina Point, just south of Malindi, the sea is encroaching on the grove of casuarina trees in spite of the breakwaters which have been built.

A fast-running sand crab, which is seldom abroad by day—they live mostly in holes which they dig in the sandy beach; and a cushion starfish or cake urchin of the family *Clypeasroidae*.

*Archie Ritchie with a tame pouch rat called 'Buku'*     *Starfish in a reef pool at Malindi*

*Portrait of a lilac-breasted roller*

*A replete toad (Bufo regularis)*

Fruit bats roosting about fifteen feet from the ground under the thick leaves of a wild almond tree, *Terminalia catappa*. For photography we illuminated them from below with a mirror.

An orb-spinning spider of the family *Argiopidae*, and below a termite, *Amitermes atlanticus*, which has just shed its wings after its one night of flight.

*A six-inch millipede*

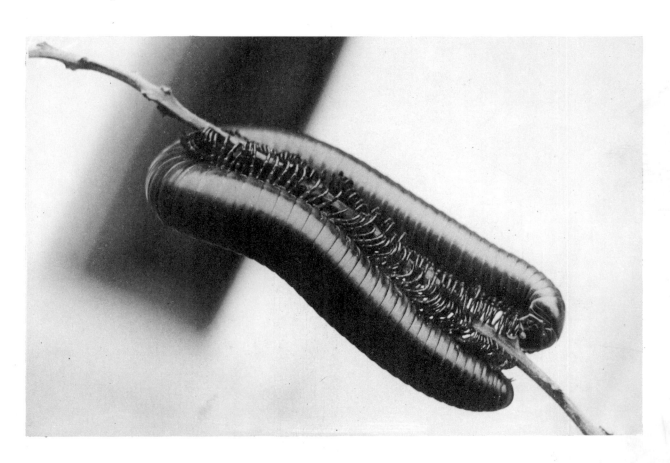

A male rhinoceros beetle, *Oryctes boas*. Several specimens all carried a cluster of mites living in the central depression of the thorax just below the tip of the horn.

A charming gecko (*Lygodactylus*) with pale blue and black stripes on its head. It is diurnal and lives mainly on the trunks of trees. The adult is about three-and-a-half inches long; the young one on my finger was much smaller.

*A flying gurnard (Dactyloptera orientalis)*

This fish was in five feet of water and spread its pectoral fins, suddenly showing a blue patch in order to discourage one from a closer approach.

*Damsel fishes (Abudefduf sexfasciatus) on the coral reef at Malindi*

*Immature angel fish (Pomacanthus semicirculatus)*

*The Coral Gardens at Malindi, with striped damsel fishes (Abudefduf sexfasciatus)*

*Lesser flamingos flighting to the freshwater spring—Nakuru*

# Lake Nakuru

# Lake Nakuru

The prime object of our trip had been to accept the invitation to perform an opening ceremony at the newly declared National Park of Lake Nakuru, the first National Park in Africa to be devoted mainly to the preservation of birds—of Nakuru's famous flamingos. At the time we were there the lake was, of course, very low because of the drought and there were said to be fewer flamingos than usual—but in spite of that they ringed the lake with a pink border visible ten miles away, and great numbers were scattered across the shallow centre. Lake Nakuru is about seven miles long and three miles wide and the flamingos—all lesser flamingos—were in every part of it, though more concentrated round some parts of the shore than others. Any estimate of the total numbers could not, in the time available to us, be better than a wild guess. Using all our experience of counting geese and trying in a rather unscientific way not to be accused of exaggerating, we concluded that there could not be less than 500,000, and the probable figure was over a million. The thickest concentration was round a freshwater spring in the north-east corner of the lake—a part which had regrettably been excluded from the Park in the interests of local sportsmen, but which it is hoped will be incorporated in due course, not only because it affords the best opportunity for watching flamingos at close range, but also because it harbours the last remaining handful of hippos on the lake.

On the morning of our arrival at Nakuru we were taken down to the edge of the lake where the opening ceremony was to be held the same evening. The strong north-east wind was whipping up clouds of white soda dust from the exposed parts of the lake bed. As we stood beside the platform which was being set up for the ceremony it was like a wartime smoke screen. The swirling clouds were acrid and pungent. Happily by the evening the wind had eased and the dust storms were less frequent. The Governor, Sir Patrick Renison, arrived with the Mayor of Nakuru and we all mounted the rostrum. The speeches were short and I made a plea for the inclusion in the Park of 'the best bit', the area nearest to Nakuru which included the freshwater spring. I cut a tape, Mervyn Cowie proposed a vote of thanks in a witty speech, and then we all set off by car on a tour of inspection. I was invited to go with the Governor in his beautiful new official Rolls-Royce and away we sped along the dried-up bed of the lake, close to the water as the ground was hard and dry. In a few minutes we had passed 50,000 flamingos. After a couple of miles we turned and this time Mervyn, with Philippa in his car, led the way, so that we might go a little closer to the water. In theory if he got stuck, the Governor's car could stop in time and turn inland on to harder ground. All went well (except for the choking soda dust which seeped into the car) until we were almost back to our starting point, when Mervyn came to a soft patch. He turned inland, but it got worse and in a moment he was bogged. We turned short and stopped just in time. Mervyn walked over to say good-bye to the Governor, who was due to set off at once for Nairobi. Then came the job of extricating Mervyn's car. A police Land Rover arrived with fifty yards of rope, but it parted every time it took the strain; at last with many people pushing as well we managed to get her out—only just in time for a lecture I was scheduled to give in Nakuru's Town Hall.

The following day, 15th February 1961, is described in my diary as 'A Flamingo Day'. Before sunrise we were driven out by Norman Jarman, who had played a leading part in getting the lake declared as a National Park, to the freshwater spring in the north-east corner where the greatest concentration of flamingos was then to be seen. Coming down towards the spring we passed a herd of nearly a hundred impala, some guinea fowl, and a single male waterbuck. In the pool of the spring were six of the last remaining hippos. We waded, almost to the top of borrowed Wellingtons, through soft mud and a bed of tall reed mace till we emerged at the edge into a hessian hide of fairly primitive construction, but superb situation. The cover was adequate and from its large 'windows' was a sight of incredible beauty and interest. The sun had not yet topped the hill behind us. The far shore of the lake was already sunlit, but the uncountable masses of flamingos which stretched from the extreme distance to within twenty yards of us in a solid mass, glowed pink in the blue shadow. On our right, where the stream debouched from the reeds, was a group of half a dozen Hottentot teal. Four marabou storks flapped away and cleared our immediate area of flamingos, but they were soon walking back towards us.

As the sun rose, the hill shadow came closer and closer until suddenly it cleared the nearest flamingos, now scarcely ten yards away. The brilliance of it was miraculous and breathtaking. Hundreds of acres were packed solidly with the pink birds, their legs a bright red forest in the foreground and below them the reflections of the nearest row. Streams of the birds were flighting in from far out in the lake, to settle in front of us, though there seemed hardly space for another to land. As they flew in front of us the low sun lit up a triangle of bright scarlet under their wings.

Meanwhile the nearest birds were bathing in the fresh water, which no doubt was a welcome contrast to the salty water in which they find their food.

I doubt if there is any more striking ornithological spectacle in the world than the flamingos of Lake Nakuru.

Later in the day the Jarmans motored us to Lake Elmenteita where many greater flamingos were mixed with the lessers. But as the sun set we were back at Nakuru in the hide by the spring. Against the light the flamingos looked strikingly different, though no less beautiful. As darkness fell most of them moved out to the open lake, away from the tall rushes which might hide leopards or jackals.

*Lesser flamingos (Phoeniconais minor)*

Into the north-east corner of Lake Nakuru runs a stream of fresh water from a spring, which contrasts with the waters of the rest of the lake. Although the soda lakes provide lesser flamingos with their staple diet of blue-green algae, the birds like to wash and drink in any fresh water available and vast numbers came daily to the outflow from the spring. From a hide in the edge of the reeds we could watch and photograph them from a range of about fifteen yards.

*Lesser flamingos at dawn on Lake Nakuru before the sun rose over the hill*

*Lesser flamingos at Lake Nakuru*

The numbers have been variously estimated at periods of peak population. In the mornings from the reed bed in the north-east corner of the lake the pink mass stretches almost as far as the eye can reach. That there may have been more than a million of the birds on the lake at the time we were there is possible; there can hardly have been less than half a million.

By the evening the flamingos had thinned out where the spring runs in, and the main flocks had withdrawn to roost in the centre of the lake.

*Cattle trails during the drought at Amboseli, the beginning of a dustbowl*

A small party of hippos lived in the spring—the last remaining hippos at Nakuru, surviving precariously in an isolated place. We found a small but well-marked frog, of the genus *Rana*.

A pair of red-eyed doves in a thorny acacia near Nakuru.

*Left:*
Marabou storks photographed on and around Nakuru's municipal rubbish tip.

*Right:*
On Lake Elmenteita, just south of Nakuru in the Rift Valley, there were both greater and lesser flamingos, but at the time we were there the numbers did not compare with those at Lake Nakuru. Nevertheless there were more than 40,000 at Elmenteita, of which rather less than half were greaters (*Phoenicopterus ruber roseus*).

# Amboseli

The famous black rhinoceros 'Gertie' after she had broken her front horn, with a four-year-old calf at Amboseli.

# Amboseli

On the southern border of Kenya with Tanganyika, immediately to the north of the great snow-capped crater of Kilimanjaro lies a large shallow pan called Lake Amboseli. At the time of our visit in March 1961 it was completely dry and we motored across the seven miles of its width on hard smooth sand, to be greeted on the farther 'shore' by a magnificent young rhino bull. Between the lake and the mountain there is a series of swamps based upon springs whose level had recently been raised by some seismic activity. Round these swamps the wildlife was rich, but the water had also to serve large numbers of Masai cattle.

Responsibility for this wonderful area was about to pass into the hands of the African District Council, and it was to become a Masai Game Reserve. There were many misgivings that this change would bring disaster to the very things which make Amboseli one of the great wonders of the world, the very attributes which bring tourists thousands of miles to Africa. The prolonged drought showed that some, at least, of the misgivings were alas justified. It is too soon yet to determine whether, in the long run, Amboseli can survive as a sanctuary for wild animals. It seems possible that the economic advantages to the tourist trade, coupled with the prestige value of National Parks—as a status symbol of the degree of civilization and enlightenment which has been attained by a newly emerging country, can yet save this unique place, with its exceptionally long horned black rhinos (many of them known by name, and delightfully indifferent to the presence of the visitors' cars) its elephants and giraffes, lions and zebras, antelopes and water birds, all to be seen (when the cloud is not down over the mountain-top) against the most noble and inspiring back-drop in all Africa.

On our short trip to Amboseli with Mervyn Cowie we were accompanied by John Williams—ornithologist of the Coryndon Museum in Nairobi, and one of the best field naturalists I have ever been out with. Much of our time was spent watching birds, lizards, frogs, spiders, butterflies and moths. The ducks for example were of especial interest, including migrant pintails and garganey from northern Europe, but also including such delightful local species as the tiny Hottentot teal and the strange white-backed ducks which sit motionless like frogs in the swamp making soft whistling noises.

But the rhinos were Amboseli's main glory, rhinos which had grown sufficiently accustomed to cars to disregard them and go about their business. In those National Parks and Reserves where the great mammals see enough vehicles to become habituated to them, you will sometimes hear the scornful comment 'They might as well be in a zoo'. This I believe to be a profoundly mistaken view. The only zoo-like quality is the indifference of the animals to the proximity of man (heavily disguised as part of the body of the motor-car animal). Thus the animals can be watched at close range going about their business in an absolutely normal and natural way. In those areas where they are not habituated to cars, they will be seen either standing wide-eyed looking at the strange beast, or galloping precipitately away. To the discerning observer this is far less satisfactory, even though the animals appear to be retaining their traditional wildness. The tameness of the National Parks is only irksome to the visitor who is more concerned with the relationship between man and animal than with the beauty and interest of the animal itself living its life undisturbed by his presence. If man had not from immemorial times been a dangerous killer, all animals would be tame to him. The fear of him which most animals show is instinctive. How easily it can be broken down is being demonstrated in many a nature reserve the world over.

*Black rhinos at Amboseli*

Extensively poached for the mythical aphrodisiac properties of rhino horn, there are, by the most optimistic estimate, no more than 13,500 black rhinos alive today. On the left they are carrying red-billed oxpeckers.

Elephant, zebras and wildebeest at Amboseli,
at the northern foot of Kilimanjaro.

*Four gazelles—all to be found at Amboseli.*
Top left, the long-necked and long-legged gerenuk—
the rarest; top right, impala; bottom left, Grant's
gazelle, showing the characteristic white 'yoke'
above the tail which most clearly distinguishes it
from the smaller Thompson's gazelle (bottom
right). All the animals on these two pages are
rams.

*A young ostrich*

*Ram Thompson's gazelle—Amboseli*

*Red-billed pintails at Amboseli, with a few Hottentot teal and a black-winged stilt on the left*

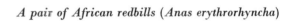

*A pair of African redbills (Anas erythrorhyncha)*

*Superb glossy starling and young—Amboseli*

*Crowned cranes at Amboseli*

*Above:*
Kori bustard male. This is the largest of the African bustards.

*Below:*
Hartlaub's bustard, taking off.

*Galeodes*—a very active spider which lives largely on white ants and belongs to the family *Solpugidae*. This female was about two-and-a-half inches long, and apricot coloured. She had a soft and flabby abdomen, huge independently operating jaws, and greatly enlarged palps which gave her, in effect, ten legs instead of eight. The heartbeats could easily be seen through the skin. The eyes were very close together and the animal's general appearance though rather horrific was somehow vaguely pathetic. The long yellow hairs are said to break off and cause a serious rash if the spider is handled, but I took no harm from allowing it to run over my hand so as to give scale to the photographs.

The silver-spotted blue *Aphnaeus hutchinsoni crucei*, a Lycaenid butterfly with well-developed 'tails' on the hind wing which take the form of false antennae. The insect usually rests head downwards. A bird seeing the slight movement of the hind wings, which it continually makes, would be encouraged to seize the false head, and be left with only a piece of the hind wings. The larva feeds on *Loranthus*—a parasitic mistletoe—being amazingly well camouflaged. In its final stages it descends to the ground where it is found by a certain species of ant for which it exudes a sweet sticky substance. The ants take it to the nest, and in return for the 'honey' they bring their own larvae on which the caterpillar feeds. It pupates in the ant's nest from which the butterfly emerges in due course.

A moth—*Sesquialtera ridicula* which mimics the characteristic double thorns of some species of acacia. The fore-wing is rolled up when the insect is in repose. This one fluttered down on to the dinner table at Amboseli.

A young bat-eared fox which was a house pet of the Warden—Colonel Taberer. It is seen in close-up on the next page.